Fact Finders®

ENERGY REVOLUTION

SOLAR ENERGY

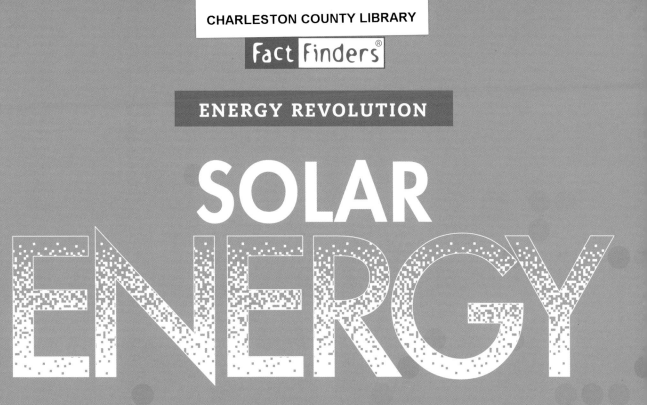

By Karen Latchana Kenney

Consultant: Ellen Anderson
Executive Director of the Energy Transition Lab
Institute on the Environment
University of Minnesota, Twin Cities

CAPSTONE PRESS
a capstone imprint

Fact Finders Books are published by Capstone Press,
1710 Roe Crest Drive, North Mankato, Minnesota 56003
www.capstonepub.com

Library of Congress Cataloging-in-Publication Data
Names: Kenney, Karen Latchana, author.
Title: Solar energy / by Karen Latchana Kenney.
Description: North Mankato, Minnesota : Capstone Press, [2019] | Series:
Fact Finders. Energy revolution | Audience: Ages 9. | Audience: Grade 4 to 6. |
   Includes bibliographical references and index.
Identifiers: LCCN 2018040986 (print) | LCCN 2018042524 (ebook) |
ISBN 9781543555462 (eBook PDF) | ISBN 9781543555400 (library binding) |
ISBN 9781543559064 (pbk.)
Subjects: LCSH: Solar energy—Juvenile literature.
Classification: LCC TJ810.3 (ebook) | LCC TJ810.3 .K46 2019 (print) | DDC
   333.792/3—dc23
LC record available at https://lccn.loc.gov/2018040986

Editorial Credits
Mandy Robbins, editor; Terri Poburka, designer; Jo Miller, media researcher;
Kathy McColley, production specialist

Photo Credits
iStockphoto: duncan1890, 14, Flairimages, 29; Newscom: Reuters/Hugh Gentry, 27;
Shutterstock, 7, Christine Bird, 16 (bottom), Costazzurra, 10, grbender, 16 (top), Hampi,
17 (bottom), iinspiration, 24-25, leungchopan, 20, Mega Pixel, 17 (top), MrNovel, 18, Piotr
Zajda, 23, Rich Carey, 21, Rosa Frei, 8-9, science photo, 28 (top), sdecoret, 4-5, Serp, 26,
SkyPics Studio, 6, Soonthorn Wongsaita, Cover, Suwin, 28 (bottom), Thomas Barrat, 12,
Tom Grundy, 11 (bottom), Wolfgang Zwanzger, 22; Wikimedia: NASA/Crew of STS-132, 19

Design Elements
Shutterstock: HAKKI ARSLAN, T.Sumaetho

Printed and bound in the USA.
PA48

TABLE OF CONTENTS

CHAPTER 1

SUN POWER

It warms the earth so that life can thrive. It helps plants grow with its beaming rays of light. It affects the weather and lights up our days. It's also free and always turned on. What is this incredible, **renewable** power source? The sun! Its power is solar energy.

The sun is our **solar system's** star. It is 93 million miles (150 million kilometers) from Earth. From there, it sends out energy every second of each day. It's been doing this for 4.5 billion years. How? The sun is a hot ball of burning gases—mostly hydrogen gas. This gas fuels the sun's power at its center, the core.

The sun has a strong force of **gravity**. Its temperature reaches 27 million degrees Fahrenheit (15 million degrees Celsius). Pressure is also strong in the core. Both the temperature and pressure change the hydrogen gas. Its atoms join together, or fuse, in the core. As they fuse, they become helium gas. But they also release energy. This process is called **nuclear fusion**.

....

renewable—describes power from sources that you can use over and over again that cannot be used up, such as wind, water, and the sun

solar system—the sun and the objects that move around it; our solar system has eight planets

gravity—a force that pulls objects together

nuclear fusion—the joining of two nuclei, which creates energy

The released energy moves very slowly through the sun's layers. Scientists think it takes more than 170,000 years for it to travel through the largest layer of the sun. This layer is called the radiative zone. Then the energy enters space as **electromagnetic radiation**. This energy contains light, X-rays, radio waves, and more. The energy rays spread out in every direction. They hit all the planets in our solar system, including Earth. Our planet receives a small portion of this energy just 8 minutes and 20 seconds after it leaves the sun.

Solar Energy's Journey

Solar energy starts in the sun's core. Then it travels through the layers of the sun before it enters space.

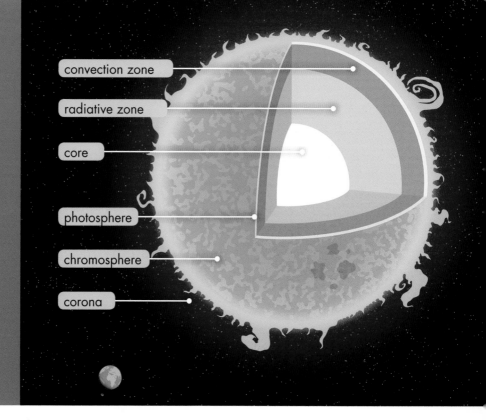

convection zone

radiative zone

core

photosphere

chromosphere

corona

As the earth's surface faces the sun, it receives the sun's energy. This energy keeps life on our planet going and growing. It warms the earth and makes air move in the **atmosphere**, creating weather patterns. Plants use the energy to make food and grow. Animals and people eat those plants and breathe the oxygen they make. The sun's energy can do more than keep us alive and warm the planet. We can also collect it in places that get lots of sunlight. With the right technology, we can turn the sun's power into electricity. Then we can use that electricity in our homes, businesses, and communities.

The sun's gravity keeps the planets in our solar system circling around it.

FACT

In one hour, the earth receives enough of the sun's energy to fuel the entire planet for one year. But right now, we can only collect about 1 percent of that energy to make electricity.

electromagnetic radiation—light, radio waves, microwaves, X-rays, and other forms of energy that travel at the speed of light

atmosphere—the mixture of gases that surrounds the earth

CHAPTER 2

CATCHING SOLAR ENERGY

The earth is constantly spinning. As it spins, the side facing the sun experiences daytime. That's when solar energy reaches that half of the planet.

Not all parts of the planet receive the same amount of energy. It depends on where you are. That's because the earth spins around on a tilt. One half of the planet is always farther away than the other half. As it moves around the sun, different parts of the earth get more solar energy. When it's winter somewhere, that part of the planet is tilted away from the sun. When it's summer, that part is tilted toward the sun.

The best places to capture solar energy receive lots of sunlight for many hours of the day. Some deserts are very hot and dry for most of the year. The Mojave Desert in the United States and the Sahara Desert in northern Africa are perfect places to collect solar energy. But you don't need to live in a desert to find solar energy. Anyone can collect it on a sunny day with the right technology. There are a few different ways to catch that sunlight.

THERMAL ENERGY SYSTEMS

One way to collect and use solar energy is to change sunlight into heat. Thermal energy systems can do this. They use solar panels to heat homes and businesses. The panels go on a building's roof. Then solar energy heats a liquid inside the panels. The heated liquid moves in pipes to rooms or storage tanks to heat the building.

In thermal energy systems, rooftop panels can heat an entire building.

Thermal systems can also use heat from the sun to make electricity. Solar thermal power plants collect solar energy using mirrors. The mirrors focus the energy onto a tube or a tower filled with liquid. The liquid receives this heat energy and gets very hot. The hot liquid turns water into steam. The steam then moves the blades of a **turbine**. This powers a **generator** that makes electricity.

....

turbine—a fan-like machine with blades that can be turned by a moving fluid such as steam or water

generator—a machine that produces electricity by turning a magnet inside a coil of wire

How a Solar Thermal Power Plant Works

1. Sunlight hits mirrors that focus energy onto tubes. This heats liquid in the tubes.

2. The heated liquid boils water into steam inside a heat exchanger. This device transfers heat from one fluid to another, cooling off the first fluid.

3. The steam moves a turbine. Then a generator makes electricity that is sent into power lines.

mirrors

turbine

generator

heat exchanger

FACT

Long, curved mirrors can capture and focus sunlight. They make its energy 30 to 100 times stronger. They make the temperature rise up to 750°F (399°C)!

SOLAR CELLS

Another way to catch sunlight is with solar cells. They change sunlight directly into electricity. Solar cells are filled with a **conducting** material. That material allows electricity to move from one point to another. These cells are grouped together in panels. You've probably seen them on rooftops. Many panels are set up as solar **arrays**. The arrays can cover a whole roof or be set up in rows in a field. Larger arrays catch even more sunlight.

Arrays are also called solar farms.

conduct—to allow heat or electricity to pass through something easily

array—a large group of solar panels

How Solar Cells Work

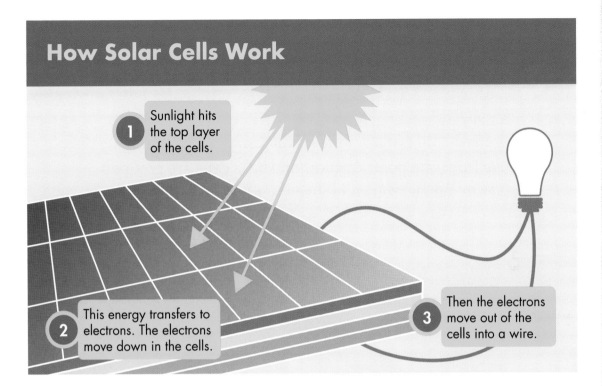

1 Sunlight hits the top layer of the cells.

2 This energy transfers to electrons. The electrons move down in the cells.

3 Then the electrons move out of the cells into a wire.

Small parts of sunlight, called **photons**, hit the tops of cells. The conducting material absorbs some of the photons. When this happens, the photons transfer energy to **electrons** in the conducting material. These electrons move down through the cells. Then the electrons move out of the cells into a wire. The wire carries the electrons in one direction. This movement of electrons is electricity.

These kinds of technology turn sunlight into energy we can use—electricity and heat. We use this electricity and heat every day in many different ways. It can keep our homes warm and our computers running.

photon—a particle or unit of light or other electromagnetic radiation

electron—a tiny particle in an atom that travels around the nucleus

CHAPTER 3

SOLAR ENERGY AT WORK

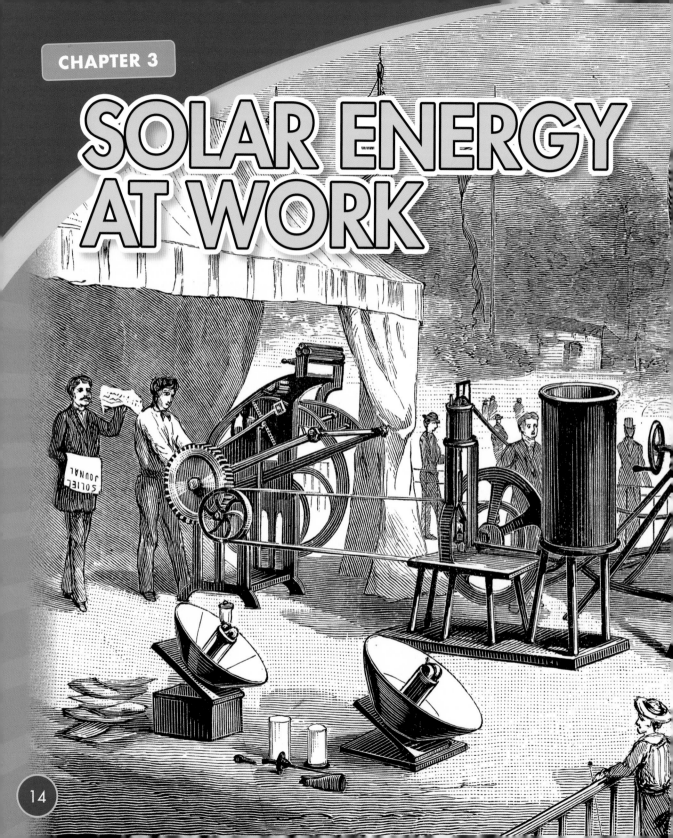

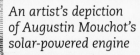
An artist's depiction of Augustin Mouchot's solar-powered engine

People have been using the sun's energy for thousands of years. Chinese, Greek, and Roman builders made houses warmed by the sun. Homes faced south so that the winter sun would heat them during the colder months. Ancient Romans used clear stone or glass on windows to trap heat inside their homes.

In 1874, French inventor Augustin Mouchot made a solar motor. It used the sun's heat to boil water. The steam powered an engine. It was the first use of solar energy to power a machine. Since then, our technology has improved.

You have probably used solar energy. Maybe you didn't even know it. Calculators were one of the first everyday products made with solar cells. Have you seen a rectangle on a calculator? That's a solar panel. It charges the calculator using sunlight. Now we use solar power in even more ways.

FACT

Solar cells can even go into clothing! These cells can bend. With the power they make, people can charge their phones.

IN THE HOME

People can use solar energy in their homes. They put solar panels on the sunniest side of their roofs. The panels provide electricity to the house. When the sun is shining, owners don't have to pay a power company for electricity. If the owner also installs an energy battery, they can charge it up when the panels produce extra electricity. The battery can use stored energy to power the home at night. Homeowners can also sell their extra electricity to a power company. The cost of installing a solar energy system in a home or building will quickly pay for itself.

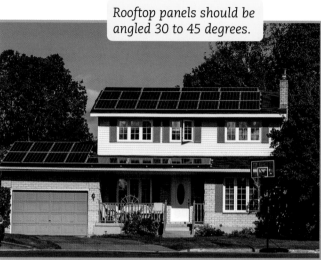

Rooftop panels should be angled 30 to 45 degrees.

Solar blankets keep pools clean and warm.

Solar power can also heat a swimming pool with a solar blanket. It is clear with lots of air pockets. It floats on top of a pool and traps the sun's heat to keep the pool water warm. Many kinds of garden lights have solar panels too. They charge up during the day. Then they turn on at night.

What's a Gigawatt?

A watt is a unit of power. It measures how much energy is used. For a 100-watt light bulb, 100 watts of electricity are used every second. In one gigawatt (GW), there are one billion watts. That's about as much power as the strength of 1.3 million horses, 5 million people riding bicycles, or 17 days worth of power used at Walt Disney World in Florida!

Top Countries for Solar Energy Use in 2017

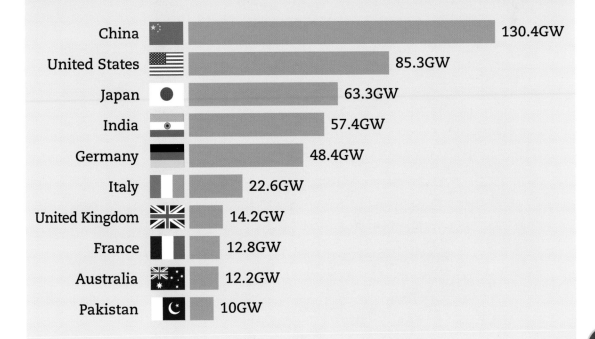

China		130.4GW
United States		85.3GW
Japan		63.3GW
India		57.4GW
Germany		48.4GW
Italy		22.6GW
United Kingdom		14.2GW
France		12.8GW
Australia		12.2GW
Pakistan		10GW

IN THE COMMUNITY

You can find solar power being used in your community too. Solar lanterns provide light. Solar batteries charge phones. Other solar-powered devices clean water for people to drink and use for cooking food. Electric road signs use solar panels. These signs tell drivers how fast they are going or how much traffic they can expect on their route.

Solar power plants make electricity that flows into power lines. Some people cannot afford to install solar panels on their homes. Instead, they can pay to get electricity from a community solar power plant.

Solar energy also helps people in places without power plants and lines. Many communities in Africa do not have easy access to electricity. With solar panels, people can charge their cell phones and power a few lights in their homes.

rooftop solar panel in South Africa

Floating Solar Farms

China uses the most solar energy of any country in the world. Chinese researchers are even finding new ways to catch sunlight. One is a solar farm filled with 166,000 panels. But these panels aren't in a field. They float on water. The lake is an old coal mine that's filled with water. This is the world's largest floating solar farm. It makes enough energy to power 15,000 homes.

FOSSIL FUELS: OUR MAIN ENERGY SOURCE

We use more solar energy than ever before. But most of our energy comes from burning fossil fuels. They include coal, natural gas, and oil. These kinds of fuels are nonrenewable. That means that there is a limited amount. Our population is growing faster than ever. We need to switch to renewable energy resources before fossil fuels run out.

Large cities throughout the world, such as Seoul, South Korea, rely heavily on fossil fuels for energy.

This coral reef has been killed by the effects of climate change. It was once teeming with life.

Using fossil fuels causes a great deal of pollution. Mining fossil fuels rips up the earth. Transporting and burning them releases carbon dioxide into the atmosphere and dangerous chemicals into the air we breathe. Too much carbon dioxide is bad for the planet. It traps heat and makes the temperature rise. The climate is already changing because of our use of fossil fuels.

Climate change affects all life on our planet. This change is especially bad for sea life. The ocean absorbs much of the planet's carbon dioxide and heat, which makes the water acidic. Higher water temperatures and acid levels kill coral reefs. The loss of coral reefs makes it harder for sea animals to breathe. It also affects the shells of some sea creatures.

SOLAR ENERGY: THE GOOD AND BAD

Solar energy is a clean energy source. We don't need to burn anything to use it, so it does not pollute the planet. Unless it's cloudy or night time, sunshine is always available. So why don't we use more of this renewable energy? There are a few reasons. In some parts of the world, the sun isn't strong enough for long periods of time. It's hard to collect enough energy for people to use.

Solar panels don't work when they're covered in snow.

Solar panel mirrors cause intensely bright reflections.

There are a few other challenges with solar technology. Some solar panels contain harmful chemicals. They need to be recycled so that these chemicals do not harm the environment. Thermal power plants can also harm birds. The bright light from the reflecting mirrors attracts insects. Birds then try to catch those insects. They fly through the intense beams of light and are killed. Engineers at power plants are still working toward a solution to this problem.

CHAPTER 4

TOMORROW'S SOLAR WORLD

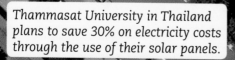

Thammasat University in Thailand plans to save 30% on electricity costs through the use of their solar panels.

The health of the entire planet depends on people finding renewable, clean energy sources. How will solar energy help us meet our future energy needs? Solar technology is improving. Solar panels are getting cheaper to make and buy. They are even less expensive than using some fossil fuels. Because of this, more and more people are putting panels on the roofs of their homes and businesses. The panels connect to **power grids** and add extra electricity that the owners do not use.

However, many power grids are not well-suited for solar energy yet. These systems of electrical lines were built to accept large amounts of power from a single source, such as a coal or nuclear power plant. With solar panels, there are many smaller sources of power going into the grid. So countries need to change their grids to "smart grids" to better accept power made by solar panels.

power grid—a network of electrical lines connecting power sources with homes and businesses over a wide area

FUTURE SOLAR TECHNOLOGIES

New building materials may make collecting solar energy even easier. Solar shingles look a lot like regular shingles. They protect buildings and make electricity too. Soon windows might be able to collect solar energy as well. Imagine skyscrapers covered in solar windows. You could still see through them, but they would also collect large amounts of energy.

In the future, skyscraper windows could collect great amounts of solar energy.

Someday we could even have a solar power plant in space. The sun always shines there! The plant could collect solar energy day and night. Satellites with large mirrors could aim sunlight onto solar panels. The panels could then turn the energy into a laser beam. The beam could travel down to the earth's surface. Then the energy could be collected and added to the power grid.

Soaring on Solar Power

The sun could even fuel airplanes one day. One airplane has already shown it's possible. It's called the *Solar Impulse 2*. Its wings and body are covered in 17,248 solar cells as thin as a human hair. The plane carries one person. Two pilots traded off flying it around the entire planet from 2015 to 2016. This technology needs to improve before regular planes can get their power from the sun. Right now, the planes need to be very lightweight.

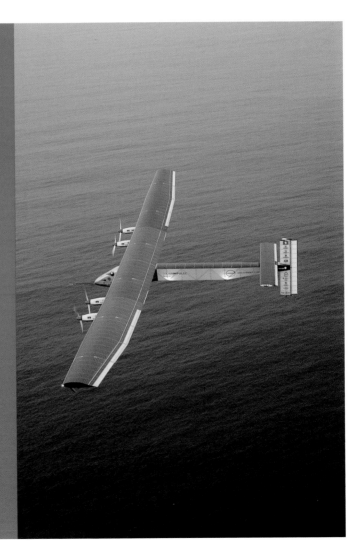

WORKING WITH SOLAR ENERGY

The future is bright in the solar energy field. Scientists are already researching metals and other materials to find better ones for solar technology. Different kinds of engineers then design the technology to use these materials in the best way possible. They also figure out ways to connect solar systems to the power grid. Installers and technicians set up solar systems in homes, businesses, and the community. Information technology (IT) specialists and software engineers work with computers to run solar energy systems.

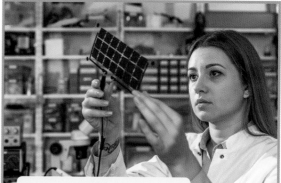

Careers in the solar energy field are varied, from engineers to installers.

The field of solar energy is growing 20 times faster than the rest of the U.S. job market. As of November 2014, there were 173,807 jobs in solar energy. Would you like to have one of those jobs some day? If you're interested in science, math, or engineering, this could be the field for you. Keep studying and learning. Get involved with your school's math league or robotics club. Maybe one day you'll be a leader in bringing solar energy to the world.

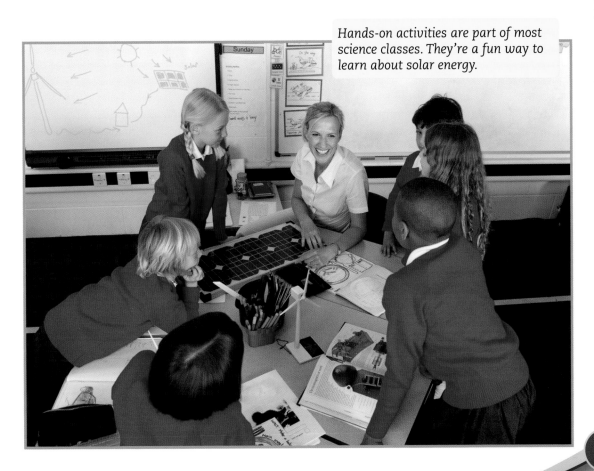

Hands-on activities are part of most science classes. They're a fun way to learn about solar energy.

GLOSSARY

array (uh-RAY)—a large group of solar panels

atmosphere (AT-muhss-fihr)—the gases that surround the earth

conduct (KON-duhkt)—to allow heat or electricity to pass through something easily

electromagnetic radiation (i-lek-troh-mag-NET-ik ray-dee-AY-shuhn)—light, radio waves, microwaves, X-rays, and other forms of energy that travel at the speed of light

electron (i-LEK-tron)—a tiny particle in an atom that travels around the nucleus

generator (JEN-uh-ray-tur)—a machine that produces electricity by turning a magnet inside a coil of wire

gravity (GRAV-uh-tee)—a force that pulls objects together

nuclear fusion (NYOO-klee-ur FYOO-shuhn)—the joining of two nuclei, which creates energy

photon (FOH-tahn)—a particle or unit of light or other electromagnetic radiation

power grid (POU-ur GRID)—a network of electrical lines connecting power sources with homes and businesses over a wide area

renewable (ri-NOO-uh-buhl)—describes power from sources that you can use over and over again that cannot be used up, such as wind, water, and the sun

solar system (SOH-lur SISS-tuhm)—the sun and the objects that move around it; our solar system has eight planets

turbine (TUR-bine)—a fan-like machine with blades that can be turned by a moving fluid such as steam or water

READ MORE

Brearley, Laurie. *Solar Power.* A True Book. New York: Children's Press, 2018.

Sawyer, Ava. *Human Environmental Impact: How We Affect Earth.* Humans and Our Planet. North Mankato, Minn.: Capstone Publishing, 2018.

Zora Scibilia, Jade. *Solar Panels: Harnessing the Power of the Sun.* Powered Up! A STEM Approach to Energy Sources. New York: PowerKids Press, 2018.

INTERNET SITES

Use FactHound to find Internet sites related to this book.

Visit www.facthound.com

Just type in 9781543555400 and go.

Super-cool stuff!

Check out projects, games and lots more at
www.capstonekids.com

CRITICAL THINKING QUESTIONS

1. In Chapter 1, the author discusses how the sun's energy benefits the planet. Can you think of some other ways people benefit from the sun's energy?

2. You learned about photons in Chapter 2. Explain what they are in your own words.

3. Using fossil fuels causes climate change. But using solar energy does not affect the climate. Can you describe some other differences between energy made from fossil fuels and energy made from the sun?

INDEX